To Kirk

Living on Cape Cod, perhaps
you can harvest some
cranberries.

Love
Gram

THE CRANBERRY COOKBOOK

THE CRANBERRY
COOKBOOK

First published in 1998
by Hamlyn
an imprint of Octopus Publishing Group Limited
2-4 Heron Quays, London E14 4JP

ISBN 0 600 59646 X

Printed in Hong Kong

Photographer: Philip Webb
Home Economist: Oona van den Berg

Contents

THE CRANBERRY COOKBOOK

In 1620, when the Pilgrim Fathers first landed on the shores of Cape Cod, Massachusetts, starvation threatened their survival until the Native Americans showed them how to live on indigenous plants and animals. One of those was the cranberry which, with its tangy taste, rich red color, and firm skin, has since found a place in the hearts and heritage of the American people. Cranberries are traditionally served with roast turkey at Thanksgiving, Christmas, and Easter, but this book proves that cranberries play a far more important role in many cuisines than merely a sauce for turkey. Fresh cranberries, cranberry sauce, and cranberry juice are becoming versatile and popular ingredients, adding their distinctive piquancy, color, and texture to savory dishes, desserts, drinks, and preserves.

History

Cranberries played an important part in Native American culture, not only because they are highly nutritious, but also because of their supposed healing properties. They bathed cuts and scratches in cranberry juice and brewed cranberry poultices to draw poison from arrow wounds. They were also used as a rich red dye for feathers, clothes, and blankets.

According to an old legend, cranberries first arrived in Cape Cod by the intervention of a white dove. During a disagreement, a medicine man cast a spell and trapped the Reverend Richard Bourne in quicksand. To settle their dispute, the two men agreed to a 15 day battle of wits. Although he was unable to move, the Reverend Bourne was kept alive by a white dove which brought him a red berry from time to time. The medicine man could not cast a spell on the dove and, exhausted, he finally fell to the ground, releasing the spell on Reverend Bourne. During the battle, one of the berries fell to the ground and germinated, creating the first of Cape Cod's cranberry bogs.

Once they had been introduced to the cranberry by the friendly native Americans, the Pilgrim women applied their own culinary know-how to developing sweetened preserves, tarts, and cranberry sauces. To celebrate their survival of the first winter, the Pilgrim Fathers and Native Americans feasted on wild turkey, cranberries, squash, and cornbread in their first Thanksgiving Feast.

Wild cranberries remained popular fruits as the small Pilgrim settlements gradually became thriving towns. Each fall, families gathered enough berries to preserve for the long winter ahead. In 1773, one Cape Cod community decreed a fine of a dollar for anyone who picked more than one quart of cranberries before September 20. In addition to losing a dollar, anyone who picked the berries too early also lost their ration of cranberries.

During the days of clipper ships and long whaling voyages, American sailors ate cranberries to ward off scurvy. The cranberries contained vital vitamin C and their natural waxy coating aided preservation over long periods at sea.

In 1844, a barrel of cranberries, which was en route to an American visitor in Hamburg, was involved in a shipwreck off the coast of Holland. The barrel floated to the island of Terschelling, where it was discovered by a beachcomber named Jan Sipkes Cupido. He was disappointed at the contents of the barrel and scattered the cranberries over the ground, taking only the barrel away with him. Flood waters later washed the discarded cranberries into low-lying areas where they germinated and flourished. Cranberries still grow today on Terschelling, but refuse to grow anywhere else in Holland.

The Crane Berry

The Pilgrims gave the cranberry its modern name. To them, the pink cranberry blossoms looked like the heads of cranes, which gorged themselves on the fruits. The name crane berry later became cranberry. Another name is bearberry because bears were also said to enjoy the succulent red fruits.

The Written Word

Cranberries have appeared in literature since as far back as the sixteenth century. The first written reference that still exists today is by James White Norwood in 1550 who referred to the Native Americans making use of cranberries. In 1605, James Rosier, in his book *The Land of Virginia*, describes the Native Americans presenting him with bark cups full of berries as he came ashore. By 1663, a recipe for cranberry sauce appeared in *The Pilgrim Cook Book*, while in 1672, John Josselyn wrote a book called *New England Rareties Discovered* and described cranberries as:

'Sauce for the Pilgrims – Cranberry or Bearberry, (because Bears use much to feed upon them) is a small trayling plant that grows in salt marshes that are over-grown with moss. The berries are of a pale yellow color, afterwards red, as big as a cherry, some perfectly round, others oval, all of them hollow with sower astringent taste; they ripen in August and September. They are excellent against the Scurvy. They are also good to allay the fervor of hoof-Diseases

'The Indians and English use them much, boyling them with sugar for Sauce to eat with their meat; and it is a delicate Sauce, especially with Roasted Mutton. Some make tarts with them as with Gooseberries.'

Cranberries entered the political arena in 1787 when Thomas Madison wrote to James Jefferson, who was in France, asking him for information to use at the Constitutional Convention. Jefferson sent over a number of useful books and, in return, asked for a gift of some pecans, Pippin apples, and cranberries.

In 1860, Edward Watson, a friend of Henry David Thoreau, wrote a poem entitled *The Cranberry Tart*, which goes as follows:

Dear Jennie, that nice cranberry tart
You gave me all bedecked with paste
Lies bleeding like a broken heart
Whose inner life has run to waste.

You placed it on the basket top,
In paper coverings still it lay.
Mid rolling seas a lurch it got
And bled its inner life away.

Its fate how like the bouyant heart
That o'er life's billowy ocean springs
Till disappointment tips the bark
And, overstrained, snap go the springs!

Cultivation

Cranberry cultivation was first recorded in 1816 in Dennis, on Cape Cod. Henry Hall noticed that the berries grew larger where the soil was covered with a layer of sand. As the berries became larger, their cultivation spread to New Jersey, Wisconsin, Washington State, and Oregon. Half of all cranberries are still grown in Massachusetts. These are all still important cranberry growing areas today.

Cranberries grow on vines in bogs and marshes built on former peat swamps. The land is drained, then cleared and levelled before a layer of sand and the vine cuttings are set in. The combination of an acid soil, the sand, and a supply of fresh water is ideal for cranberry growing. It takes from three to five years from the planting of a bog to the first harvest, but once started, vines will produce fruit almost indefinitely. Vines are pruned in spring and autumn and weeded during the summer months. By July, they are covered with pale pink blossom.

The berries start to form after the flowers fade, and by fall, the cranberry bogs are glowing scarlet. If frost threatens as harvest time approaches, the bogs are flooded overnight. They are also flooded during the winter months to protect the vines from cold weather, but in the warmer summer weather, they are allowed to dry out. Labor Day usually signifies the start of the harvest season and the fresh berries are available right through to December.

Harvesting

Cranberries are harvested by one of two methods: dry harvesting and wet harvesting. Fruit that is destined to be sold as fresh berries is dry harvested. Mechanical pickers are driven around the bogs, combing the berries from the vines with metal teeth. A conveyor belt carries the fruit to a box or bag at the back of the machine. Fruit that is destined to be made into sauces or juice is wet harvested. The bogs are flooded to a depth of about 18 inches and a machine, rather like a lawn tractor, churns up the water enough to dislodge the berries, making them float to the surface. The berries are then gathered using floating booms and conveyed to trucks on dry land.

The berries are taken to a central processing plant where they are cleaned with water and airstreams to remove pieces of leaf or stem. The clean berries are then passed through metal sieves to grade them according to size.

The quality of each cranberry destined to be sold fresh, rather than being processed, is tested by bouncing it on a hard surface. The berries have to bounce over a four-inch wooden barrier, seven times, before they pass the test; if they don't they are discarded. Because of this test and the berry's ability to bounce, the cranberry gets yet another of its names, the bounceberry.

Cranberries and Health

Like most fruits, cranberries are low in fat and high in dietary fibre, but they are also very rich in vitamin C, making them a valuable part of anyone's diet. Scientists have also found that cranberry juice seems to prevent certain bacteria clinging to the insides of the bladder and urinary tract, so preventing bladder infections and cystitis to which many women are prone.

Cranberries in the Kitchen

Fresh cranberries will keep well in a refrigerator for up to 4 weeks in an unopened bag, or up to 10 days once opened, as long as any damaged fruit has been removed first.

To prepare the fresh berries, remove all the stalks and any leaves, if necessary, then rinse well under cold running water and carefully pat them dry.

Fresh cranberries are available from September to

December. As the season is so short, it is well worth freezing some fresh berries for use at a later date. They will keep for up to a year if they are well sealed in plastic bags. Cranberries can also be bought ready-frozen and it is sometimes possible to buy them in cans, too, but they lose some of their texture during the canning process, so buy fresh or frozen ones if possible.

Cranberries are also now available dried. Dried berries are rather tart with an intense fruitiness, and are delicious used in sauces, stuffings, breakfast cereals, and for baking. They can be used in exactly the same way as raisins and are equally delicious eaten straight from the bag as a snack.

Cooking with Cranberries

Their wonderfully tart, piquant flavor makes cranberries suitable for both sweet and savory dishes. This book offers a whole host of very diverse recipes for starters, main courses, desserts, and drinks featuring cranberries. Try them with apples in a tart (see page 34), or in muffins (see page 46). They also make lovely ice creams and sorbets (see page 41). Cranberries are natural partners to many meats and poultry; (see the Main Courses chapter on page 12).

Hints, Tips and Great Ideas

When making sweet dishes with cranberries, cook the berries in liquid until they pop before you add the sugar, otherwise the skins of the cranberries will remain tough.

A few lightly cooked cranberries can be added to gravies to accompany roast meats, or stir into casseroles containing duck, game, goose, lamb, or chicken.

Use fresh or dried cranberries in place of raisins or sultanas as a fruity filling for baked apples.

Ready made cranberry sauce makes an unusual topping for a winter pavlova or cheesecake. Also try it as a filling for scones, cakes, and pastries.

Add a few dried cranberries to a sweetened oil and vinegar dressing for a warm meat or poultry salad.

The high pectin content of cranberries makes them ideal for use in jams and jellies. Combine with sweeter fruits for best results. The list of possible combinations is endless.

When making your own cranberry sauce or relish, try adding orange zest, cloves, red wine, port, or fruit liqueur for a dash of luxury.

Use a spoonful of cranberry sauce to add a touch of zest in toasted sandwich fillings with cheese, ham or bacon.

Transform a shepherd's pie with a tablespoon of cranberry sauce stirred into the meat mixture to add a tangy flavour.

Cranberry jelly makes a great glaze for fruit tarts or flans. Warm gently and brush over the surface for a glossy finish.

Stir-fries are becoming increasingly popular as quick and healthy dishes. Add a spoonful of cranberry sauce towards the end of cooking to give a fresh, sweet taste.

Melted cranberry sauce or jelly makes a great sauce for ice cream. Add a dash of liqueur or orange juice for a more sophisticated sauce.

Sprinkle dried cranberries on breakfast cereals, muesli, yogurt, or salads for a tangy taste and chewy texture.

CRANBERRY DUCK

4½–6 pound duck
⅔ cup chicken stock or canned broth
2–3 tablespoons cranberry sauce
2–3 tablespoons port
4½ teaspoons grated orange zest
⅓ cup orange juice
2 tablespoons plus 2 teaspoons lemon juice
1½ teaspoons cornstarch
salt and pepper
orange segments, to garnish

1 Preheat the oven to 375°F. Dry the duck thoroughly inside and out with paper towels. Prick the duck all over with a fork and place on a rack in a roasting pan. Sprinkle lightly with salt.
2 Roast for about 25 minutes per pound or until cooked through, basting once during cooking. Increase the oven temperature to 400°F for the last 10 minutes of cooking.
3 Transfer the duck to a serving dish and cover and keep warm. Drain off all the fat from the pan, leaving the juices. Combine the stock or canned broth, cranberry sauce, port, orange zest, juice, and lemon juice and pour into the pan. Bring to the boil, stirring frequently and scraping up the brown bits from the bottom of the pan. Simmer for 2–3 minutes.
4 Blend the cornstarch with a little cold water to make a smooth paste. Stir into the pan and simmer for a further 2–3 minutes until the sauce has thickened. Season to taste. Pour the sauce into a warmed sauceboat.
5 Garnish the duck with orange segments and serve with the sauce handed round separately. Roast potatoes and steamed broccoli would make good accompaniments.

Serves 4
Preparation time: 5 minutes
Cooking time: 1¼–2 hours

TURKEY IN A BRICK WITH CRANBERRIES AND ORANGE

1½ cups cranberries, defrosted, if frozen
3 tablespoons grated orange zest
⅓ cup orange juice
2 tablespoons light brown sugar
2–3 sprigs of thyme, plus extra to garnish
¼ cup butter
4 pound turkey, giblets removed
salt and pepper

1 Preheat the oven to 450°F. Prepare the brick according to the manufacturer's instructions. Place the cranberries in the bottom half, then add the orange zest, juice, and sugar. Stir well. Place the sprigs of thyme on top.

2 Soften the butter and season to taste. Lift the skin away from the turkey breast and spread the butter all over the flesh. Press the skin back into place.

3 Put the turkey, breast-side up, on the bed of cranberries. Season to taste. Cover with the top half of the brick and place in the oven. Bake for exactly 2 hours without opening the oven door.

4 Lift the turkey out of the brick and place on a warmed serving platter. Remove the cranberries with a slotted spoon and arrange around the turkey. Garnish with thyme and serve the juices separately.

Serves 4
Preparation time: 10 minutes
Cooking time: 2 hours

13

GLAZED TURKEY BREASTS
WITH CRANBERRY AND CHESTNUT STUFFING

4 turkey breast fillets, 5 ounces each
2 tablespoons vegetable oil, for frying
1 tablespoon sugar
1¼ cups cranberry juice
¼ cup cranberries, defrosted, if frozen
salt and pepper
sprig of thyme, to garnish

Stuffing:
1 large onion, finely chopped
2 tablespoons vegetable oil, for frying
1 pound turkey or pork mince
1 cup fresh white bread crumbs
1 cup canned chestnuts, chopped
¼ cup dried cranberries
1 teaspoon chopped fresh thyme
2 teaspoons chopped fresh sage
1 egg, beaten

1 Preheat the oven to 400°F. Grease a 1-lb loaf pan.
2 To make the stuffing, lightly fry the onion in the oil until golden brown. Stir in the mince and bread crumbs and cook for 2–3 minutes. Add the chestnuts, dried cranberries, thyme, and sage. Mix together well and season to taste. Remove from the heat and stir in the beaten egg. Spoon into the loaf pan and cook on the middle shelf of the oven for 1 hour, or until the top is a rich golden brown.
3 Season the turkey fillets on both sides and then lightly fry in the oil until golden brown. Add the sugar and cranberry juice to the pan, cover, and simmer gently for 15 minutes. Add the cranberries and cook for a further 5 minutes, or until the turkey has cooked through and the berries have slightly softened.
4 Remove the stuffing from the pan and cut into 8 thick slices. Serve the turkey fillets either whole or sliced and arranged over two slices of stuffing on each plate. Bring the cranberry sauce to the boil for 5 minutes or until thickened and pour over the turkey. Serve with green beans and snow peas and garnish with thyme.

Serves 4
Preparation time: 20 minutes
Cooking time: 1 hour 30 minutes

VENISON CASSEROLE WITH CRANBERRY DUMPLINGS

2½ pounds stewing venison, cut into 1–1½ inch cubes
2 tablespoons all-purpose flour
3 tablespoons olive oil
6 ounces smoked bacon, cut into strips
2 onions, chopped
2 garlic cloves, crushed
1¾ cups chicken stock or canned broth
1 sprig rosemary
1 sprig thyme
1 bay leaf
6 juniper berries, crushed
salt and pepper

Marinade:
1¼ cups red wine
1 onion, chopped
3 tablespoons Cognac
2 tablespoons olive oil

Cranberry dumplings:
¼ cup cranberries, defrosted, if frozen
1 tablespoon sugar
1 tablespoon water
1 cup self-rising flour, sifted
½ cup fresh white bread crumbs
1 ounce shredded suet
2 tablespoons chopped fresh parsley

1 Place the cubes of venison in a large bowl, add the marinade ingredients, stir well, cover, and leave to marinate in the refrigerator for 12–24 hours.

2 Remove the venison pieces from the marinade and pat dry. Strain the marinade through a strainer. Discard the onion and reserve the marinade liquid. Season the flour and roll the meat in it, shaking off any excess.

3 Heat the oil in a flameproof casserole over a moderate heat, add the venison in batches, and brown well all over. Remove the meat with a slotted spoon and set aside.

4 Add the bacon to the casserole dish and cook for 3–4 minutes until lightly browned. Add the onions and garlic and cook for 8–10 minutes until softened. Pour in the reserved marinade liquid, bring to the boil, and boil rapidly until reduced by one-third.

5 Return the venison to the casserole dish along with any juices. Stir in the stock or canned broth, rosemary, thyme, bay leaf, and juniper berries. Bring to the boil, cover tightly, and simmer gently for 1½–2 hours until the meat is tender. Alternatively, cook in a preheated oven at 325°F.

6 To make the dumplings, place the cranberries and sugar in a small saucepan with the water. Bring to the boil and simmer gently for 1–2 minutes until the berries start to char.

7 Mix the flour, bread crumbs, suet and parsley together in a bowl. Season to taste. Stir in the cranberries, adding more water, if needed, to make a soft dough. Form into 8 small balls and add to the casserole for the last 15–20 minutes of cooking time. Cover and cook until the dumplings are risen and fluffy. Remove the bay leaf from the casserole and serve.

Serves 4
Preparation time: 35 minutes, plus marinating
Cooking time: 1¾–2¼ hours

CRANBERRY BAKED HAM

5 pound ham, boned and rolled
1 bay leaf
½ small onion, peeled
1 carrot, sliced
3 cloves
½ teaspoon black peppercorns
2 tablespoons light brown sugar
¼ cup cranberry sauce
2 tablespoons whole grain mustard
½ teaspoon allspice
¼ teaspoon ground coriander
fresh cranberries, to garnish

1 Soak the ham overnight in cold water. (If this is not possible, place the ham in a large saucepan of cold water and bring to the boil. Remove the ham, discard the water.)

2 Place the ham in a pan of cold, fresh water. Add the bay leaf, onion, carrot, cloves, and peppercorns. Bring to the boil, cover, and simmer for 1½ hours.

3 Preheat the oven to 425°F. Remove the ham from the water. Peel off the skin with a sharp knife, leaving the white fat.

4 Place the ham in a roasting pan. Using a knife point, score diagonal lines across the fat to make a diamond pattern.

5 Mix together the sugar, cranberry sauce, mustard, and spices. Brush the mixture into the fat. Bake the ham for 30 minutes. Serve garnished with fresh cranberries.

Serves 8–10
Preparation time: 15 minutes, plus soaking
Cooking time: 2 hours

SMOKED TURKEY AND CRANBERRY POT PIES

1 large onion, chopped
1 celery stick, chopped
2 tablespoons vegetable oil
2 tablespoons all-purpose flour
2 cups chicken stock or canned broth
1 cup heavy cream
1 tablespoon sherry
1 pound sweet potatoes, peeled and
roughly chopped
8 small shallots, peeled
8 ounces button mushrooms,
halved or sliced
12 ounces smoked turkey,
roughly chopped
2 tablespoons dried cranberries, chopped
2 tablespoons chopped fresh parsley
1 pound puff pastry
1 egg, beaten
salt and pepper

1 Preheat the oven to 450°F. Fry the onion and celery in the oil until golden brown. Add the flour and stir well. Remove from the heat and add the stock or canned broth, whisking well with a wire whisk to remove all the lumps. Return to the heat and continue whisking until smooth.

2 Add the cream and heat gently. Season to taste. Add the sherry, sweet potatoes, shallots, mushrooms, turkey, cranberries, and parsley and stir to combine. Simmer gently for 10 minutes and then leave to cool.

3 Divide the mixture between six small ovenproof dishes. Roll out the pastry to ⅛ inch thick and cut circles 1 inch wider than the diameter of the dishes. Brush the rim of each dish with a little beaten egg. Place a pastry circle on top of each dish, gently pressing the pastry around the rim to secure. Cut a small hole in each pastry lid and use any remaining pastry to make pastry leaves to decorate the lids.

4 Bake on the middle shelf of the oven for 30–35 minutes, or until the pastry is puffed and golden brown. Serve with green beans.

Serves 6
Preparation time: 40 minutes
Cooking time: 50–55 minutes

CRANBERRY PORK ROAST

2 tablespoons oil
3½ pound boneless pork shoulder roast
⅔ cup water
1½ cups cranberries, defrosted, if frozen
2 tablespoons honey
1 teaspoon finely grated orange zest
pinch of ground cloves
pinch of ground nutmeg
salt and pepper

1 Preheat the oven to 350°F.

2 Heat the oil in a skillet and brown all sides of the pork. Bring the water to a boil in a saucepan, add the cranberries, and cook for 5 minutes. Transfer the meat to a casserole dish, season with salt and pepper and spread with honey and orange zest. Sprinkle the meat with cloves and nutmeg, then pour the cranberries over the meat. Cover, and bake for 1½ hours or until the internal temperature of the meat reaches 170°F. Serve sliced, accompanied by the sauce.

Serves: 4–6
Preparation time: 10 minutes
Cooking time: 1¼ hours

PORK CHOPS WITH APPLE AND CRANBERRY SAUCE

I small red cabbage, finely shredded
I onion, thinly sliced
4 cloves
I apple, cored and sliced
¼ cup red wine vinegar
¼ cup light brown sugar
4 pork chops
2 tablespoons vegetable oil
½ cup dry red wine
8-ounce can whole berry
cranberry sauce
3 tablespoons orange zest
salt and pepper

1 Preheat the oven to 350°F. Place the red cabbage, onion, cloves, apple, red wine vinegar, and sugar in a casserole dish and season to taste. Cover and cook for 1 hour.

2 Meanwhile sauté the pork chops on both sides in the oil, until lightly browned. Add the red wine, cranberry sauce, and orange zest and season with salt and pepper to taste. Cover and simmer gently for about 40 minutes, or until the pork chops are tender and glazed.

3 Serve the pork chops accompanied by the red cabbage.

Serves 4
Preparation time: 10 minutes
Cooking time: 1 hour

CRANBERRY CHICKEN STIR-FRY WITH GINGER

2 tablespoons vegetable oil
2 shallots, finely chopped
1 inch piece of fresh ginger root, peeled and thinly sliced into julienne strips
2 garlic cloves, crushed
4 skinless chicken breasts, about 3 ounces each, thinly sliced
2 tablespoons hoisin sauce
2 tablespoons oyster sauce
1 tablespoon light soy sauce
¼ cup dried cranberries
4 green onions (scallions), diagonally sliced
2 cups beansprouts, or sliced green or red bell pepper or carrot strips

To garnish:
vegetable oil, for deep frying
handful of basil leaves
1 large red chili pepper, deseeded and finely sliced

1 Heat the 2 tablespoons of oil in a wok and stir-fry the shallots, ginger, and garlic for 30 seconds. Add the chicken and stir-fry for 2 minutes or until golden brown.

2 Add the hoisin, oyster, and soy sauces and the cranberries and stir-fry for a further 2 minutes. Check that the chicken is cooked all the way through, then add the green onions and beansprouts or other vegetables, if using, and toss together for 3–4 minutes.

3 In a small saucepan containing ½ inch of oil, deep fry the basil leaves and red chili in two batches for 10–30 seconds until crisp. Use the basil and chili as a garnish for the stir-fry.

Serves 4
Preparation time: 20 minutes
Cooking time: 10 minutes

LAMB WITH CRANBERRIES AND HONEY

4 lean lamb sirloin or leg steaks,
6 ounces each
⅔ cup cranberry juice
¼ cup cranberries, defrosted, if frozen
3 tablespoons honey
sprigs of mint, to garnish

1 Trim any fat from the lamb steaks and place them in a large dish. Pour over the cranberry juice. Cover and leave to marinate for at least 4 hours. Drain the meat and reserve the marinade.
2 Place the lamb steaks over a hot barbecue, or under a preheated hot broiler and cook for 7–10 minutes or until they are browned, turning them once.
3 Meanwhile, place the marinade and cranberries in a saucepan and boil rapidly for 5 minutes, or until the cranberries are soft. Add the honey and stir until it has melted.
4 Serve the lamb steaks with the cranberry sauce spooned over. Garnish with sprigs of mint.

Serves 4
Preparation time: 5–10 minutes, plus marinating
Cooking time: 7–10 minutes

CRANBERRY STEAKS

**4 sirloin steaks, about 6 ounces each
and 1 inch thick
2 tablespoons butter
1–1½ teaspoons grated lemon zest
4½ teaspoons lemon juice
12 fresh cranberries, crushed
¾ cup vegetable stock or canned broth
1 tablespoon red wine vinegar
2 tablespoons cranberry sauce
3 tablespoons heavy cream
1½ teaspoons cornstarch
salt and pepper**

1 Preheat the oven to 400°F. Trim the steaks, if necessary, and season with salt and pepper.

2 Melt the butter in a frying pan and, when really hot, add the steaks and fry to seal on both sides. Transfer to a casserole dish.

3 Add to the pan juices the lemon zest and juice, cranberries, stock or canned broth, vinegar, and cranberry sauce. Bring to the boil and boil rapidly for 2–3 minutes, scraping up the brown bits from the bottom of the pan. Season well.

4 Pour the sauce over the steaks in the casserole dish, cover and cook in the oven for 40 minutes.

5 Pour the sauce off the steaks into a small saucepan. Keep the meat covered and warm. Blend the cream with the cornstarch in a small bowl, then add a little of the sauce. Pour it all back into the pan, mix well and boil for 1 minute. Taste and adjust the seasoning if necessary.

6 Arrange the steaks in a deep serving dish and pour over the creamy cranberry sauce.

Serves 4
Preparation time: 15 minutes
Cooking time: 50 minutes

BAKED BRIE WITH CRANBERRIES

Baked Brie:
½ cup toasted fresh bread crumbs
1 tablespoon chopped parsley
1 teaspoon chopped thyme
1 tablespoon dried cranberries, finely chopped
4 x 2 ounce pieces of Brie
1 egg, beaten

Relish:
2 cups cranberries, defrosted, if frozen
3 tablespoons grated orange zest
⅓ cup orange juice
½ inch piece of fresh root ginger, peeled and grated
½ cup sugar

To serve:
arugula or assorted lettuce leaves
4 thick slices French bread, toasted
1 garlic clove, cut in half lengthways
snipped fresh chives

1 Preheat the oven to 425°F. Grease a baking sheet.
2 To make the relish, place the cranberries together with the grated orange zest and juice, ginger, and sugar, in a blender or food processor and process to a coarse purée. Leave to stand for 1 hour before serving.
3 To make the baked Brie, mix the toasted bread crumbs with the parsley, thyme, and dried cranberries. Dip each piece of Brie into the beaten egg and then coat evenly with the bread crumb mixture.
4 Place the pieces of coated Brie on the baking sheet and bake on the middle shelf of the oven for 8 minutes. Remove the Brie from the oven and leave to cool briefly.
5 Arrange the arugula or lettuce leaves on 4 plates. Spoon some cranberry relish on to the plates and place the warm Brie on slices of toasted French bread, that have been rubbed with a garlic half and extra cranberry relish. Garnish with chives.

Serves 4
Preparation time: 25 minutes, plus standing
Cooking time: 10 minutes

SMOKED TURKEY AND CRANBERRY PIZZA

Pizza base:
1 tablespoon extra-virgin olive oil
1½ cups all-purpose flour
½ teaspoon salt
1 teaspoon easy-blend yeast
⅔ cup warm water

Topping:
4 tablespoons sun-dried tomato paste
1 tablespoon chopped sage
4 ounces smoked turkey, sliced
1 red onion, thinly sliced
4 tablespoons cranberry sauce
¼ cup grated mozzarella cheese
¼ cup grated Cheddar cheese
2 tablespoons chopped basil

1 Lightly grease four baking sheets with the oil.

2 To make the pizza base sift the flour and salt together and stir in the yeast. Add enough of the warm water to create a soft dough. Knead the dough for 5–10 minutes or until smooth. Transfer to a greased bowl, cover with a damp cloth and leave for 1 hour to double in size. Preheat the oven to 450°F.

3 Knead the dough once more, then divide into four pieces. Shape and roll out each to a 6 inch circle. Place one on each baking sheet.

4 For the topping, mix together the sun-dried tomato paste with the sage and spread over the pizza bases. Arrange the slices of smoked turkey and red onion, and spoonfuls of cranberry sauce over the top of each pizza.

5 Mix together the mozzarella and Cheddar and sprinkle over the turkey and onions. Top with the basil. Bake in two batches for 10–15 minutes or until the cheese is melted and bubbling and the bases are golden brown.

Serves 4
Preparation time: 30 minutes, plus rising
Cooking time: 10–15 minutes

COUSCOUS WITH DRIED CRANBERRIES AND ORANGE ZEST

This recipe is illustrated on page 2.

½ cup couscous
10 saffron strands, soaked in 2 tablespoons boiling water
2 large onions, roughly chopped
2 tablespoons olive oil
¼ cup dried cranberries
2 tablespoons toasted, blanched almonds
½ tablespoon chopped cilantro
3 tablespoons orange zest
1 tablespoon chopped mint
salt and pepper

Yogurt dressing:
2 cups plain yogurt
2 teaspoons chili sauce
2 tablespoons olive oil
1 tablespoon lemon juice
1 tablespoon chopped mint

1 Place the couscous in a bowl and add the saffron strands and soaking liquid. Pour over enough boiling water to just cover the couscous. Leave to stand for 10 minutes to allow the couscous to soak. Toss the couscous with a fork to separate the grains then spoon into a steamer and steam for 10 minutes, or until required.

2 Lightly fry the onion in the oil until just golden brown. Add the fried onion, cranberries, almonds and cilantro to the couscous. Warm through, remove from the heat and stir in the orange zest, mint, and season to taste.

3 To make the dressing, mix together all the ingredients in a screw-top jar and serve separately. Serve as an accompaniment to grilled lamb chops or chicken breasts or as a main course with a leafy green salad.

Serves 4
Preparation time: 10 minutes, plus standing
Cooking time: 10–12 minutes

BAKED ACORN SQUASH WITH CRANBERRY STUFFING

4 small acorn squash
rice, to serve
mixed leaves, to garnish

Cranberry stuffing:
3 shallots, finely chopped
4 garlic cloves, crushed
2 tablespoons vegetable oil
I red chili, deseeded and finely chopped
I tablespoon ground cumin
I tablespoon ground coriander
I tablespoon ground cinnamon
2 teaspoons ground ginger
I cup minced pork
¼ cup pine nuts, toasted
¼ cup cranberries, defrosted, if frozen
I tablespoon chopped parsley
salt and pepper

1 Preheat the oven to 400°F. Cut off the top of the squash and scoop out the seeds, reserve the tops. Cut a slice off the bases of the squash so the shells can stand upright on a baking sheet.

2 To make the stuffing, gently fry the shallots and garlic in the oil in a frying pan until beginning to brown. Add the chili, cumin, coriander, cinnamon, and ginger to the pan and fry, stirring constantly, for about 1 minute.

3 Add the pork and nuts and fry until the meat has browned. Stir in the cranberries, and parsley. Season to taste. Remove from the heat and spoon the cranberry stuffing into the center of each squash until firmly packed.

4 Replace the lids on the squash and cook on the middle shelf of the oven for 1 hour, or until the squash are soft and cooked through and the stuffing is piping hot. Serve with rice and garnish with mixed leaves.

Serves 4
Preparation time: 25 minutes
Cooking time: 1 hour 20 minutes

WARM SPINACH SALAD WITH CRANBERRIES, WALNUTS, AND GOAT'S CHEESE

3 cups young spinach leaves
4 thick slices firm goat's cheese
4 slices French bread
¼ cup walnut pieces
2 tablespoons fresh cranberries
1 tablespoon sunflower oil

Dressing:
2 tablespoons extra-virgin olive oil
4 tablespoons balsamic vinegar
1 tablespoon very finely chopped
red bell pepper
1 garlic clove, crushed
salt and pepper

To garnish:
1 tablespoon chopped Italian or
flat-leaf parsley
chives, chopped

1 Arrange the spinach leaves over four plates. To make the dressing, put all the ingredients in a small saucepan and warm gently.

2 Preheat the broiler. Place one slice of goat's cheese on top of each slice of French bread and broil for 3–4 minutes or until just bubbling.

3 Place the walnuts in a hot frying pan and toast on all sides. Remove and reserve. Add the cranberries and the sunflower oil to the pan and quickly sear for 2–3 minutes.

4 Scatter the cranberries and walnuts over the spinach and place the bread and goat's cheese in the middle of each salad.

5 Drizzle the warm dressing over the goat's cheese and salad. Garnish with parsley and chives. Serve immediately.

Serves 4
Preparation time: 10 minutes
Cooking time: 6–8 minutes

WILD RICE WITH CRANBERRIES AND PECANS
This recipe is illustrated on page 3.

1½ cups wild rice
1 onion, finely chopped
1 garlic clove, crushed
2 tablespoons olive oil
3½ cups chicken stock or canned broth
2 teaspoons dried mixed herbs
¼ cup cranberries, defrosted, if frozen
¼ cup dried cranberries
¼ cup pecans, toasted
2 tablespoons chopped cilantro
salt and pepper

1 Rinse the wild rice thoroughly and then soak in cold water for 1 hour. Drain.

2 Fry the onion and garlic in the oil in a large saucepan until softened but not brown. Add the rice to the pan and coat in the oil. Add the stock or canned broth and dried herbs, bring to the boil, and simmer in a covered pan for 40 minutes.

3 Add the fresh and dried cranberries and pecans and simmer uncovered for a further 5–10 minutes. If any cooking liquid remains, increase the heat and boil it off. Remove from the heat and stir in the cilantro. Season to taste. Serve immediately while still warm with duck, lamb, or game. Alternatively, cool completely and serve as a salad.

Serves 4
Preparation time: 20 minutes, plus soaking
Cooking time: 1 hour

CRANBERRY-APPLE TART WITH WALNUT CRUST

Crust:
¼ **cup walnut halves, finely chopped**
6 **ounces butter**
⅓ **cup superfine sugar**
2 **cups all-purpose flour**
cold water

Sponge filling:
4 **ounces butter**
½ **cup superfine sugar**
2 **eggs, beaten**
½ **cup self-rising flour**
2 **tablespoons cranberry jelly or sauce**
1 **cooking apple, peeled, cored and sliced**
¼ **cup fresh cranberries**

1 Preheat the oven to 400°F. Grease a 10-inch pan. To make the crust, put the walnuts, butter, sugar, and flour in a food processor or bowl and mix, then add enough cold water to form a soft dough. Spoon into the pan and using the back of a spoon, press over the base and up the sides. Bake for 30 minutes, or until golden brown.

2 To make the filling, beat together the butter and sugar until soft and fluffy. Add the eggs and flour, and beat until smooth.

3 Spread the cranberry jelly or sauce over the bottom of the cooked crust, then pour the filling over and smooth the top. Scatter the apple and cranberries over the sponge mixture.

4 Reduce the oven temperature to 375°F. Bake the tart on the middle shelf of the oven for 40–50 minutes or until the filling is well risen and golden brown, and the center is firm when pressed.

Serves 6–8
Preparation time: 25 minutes
Cooking time: 1 hour 20 minutes

CRANBERRY UPSIDE-DOWN CAKE

1⅛ cups cranberries, defrosted, if frozen
⅔ cup water
½ cup butter
½ cup superfine sugar
I egg, beaten
I cup self-rising flour, sifted
3 tablespoons grated orange zest
I tablespoon orange juice
I tablespoon cranberry jelly, to glaze

1 Preheat the oven to 350°F. Put the cranberries and water into a saucepan, bring to the boil, and simmer for 5–10 minutes or until the cranberry skins begin to pop.
2 Grease and line a 7-inch round cake pan. Melt together 1 tablespoon of the butter and 1 tablespoon of the sugar and put into the pan. Add the cranberries.
3 Cream together the remaining butter and sugar until light and fluffy. Beat in the egg, then lightly fold in the flour, orange zest, and juice. Spread the mixture over the top of the cranberries.
4 Bake for 30 minutes or until the top springs back when lightly pressed. Turn out upside down on a wire rack and leave to cool.
5 Melt the jelly in a small saucepan over a gentle heat. Brush over the cranberries to glaze.

Serves 4
Preparation time: 20 minutes
Cooking time: 45 minutes

CRANBERRY APPLE STRUDELS

2 cups all-purpose flour
½ teaspoon salt
1 egg, beaten
2 tablespoons oil
⅓ cup lukewarm water
confectioner's sugar, to dredge
pinch of ground cinnamon

Filling:
2 pounds cooking apples, peeled
cored and sliced
1½ cups fresh cranberries, defrosted,
if frozen
½ teaspoon ground cinnamon
about 4 tablespoons water
sugar, to taste
¼ cup butter, melted
1¼ cups ground almonds

1 Sift together the flour and salt, make a well in the center. Add the egg, oil, and water and mix together gradually to make a soft sticky dough. Work the dough until it leaves the bowl clean.

2 Turn out on to a lightly floured surface and knead for about 15 minutes. Shape into a ball, cover with a cloth, then cover with the bowl and leave in a warm place to rest for 1 hour.

3 To make the filling, put the apples into a saucepan with the cranberries, cinnamon, and water. Cover and simmer gently for about 10 minutes, or until soft. Beat in the sugar, to taste and leave to cool completely. Warm a wooden rolling pin and spread a clean cloth on a work surface. Dredge lightly with flour.

4 Place the dough on to the cloth and roll out carefully into a square about ⅛ inch thick. Lift the dough and turn it frequently so that it does not stick to the cloth.

5 Gently slide the backs of your hands under the dough and gently lift and stretch it, beginning in the center and working out to the edge until it is paper thin and measures about 32 inches square. Neaten the edges with a sharp knife and leave to rest for 15 minutes. Brush the dough all over with most of the melted butter, then sprinkle with the almonds.

6 Preheat the oven to 375°F. Grease 2 large baking sheets.

7 Cut the dough in half and then cut each piece into four oblongs of equal size by cutting at right angles to the first cut.

8 Divide the fruit mixture between the pieces of dough, spreading it to within 1 inch of both long sides and one short side, and 3 inches of the other short side. Fold the narrow edges over the filling and, beginning at the narrow end, roll up towards the wide border, keeping it neat and even. Stand the parcels on the baking sheets, keeping the join underneath. Brush with melted butter.

9 Bake for 25–30 minutes or until golden brown. Transfer to a wire rack and leave to cool. Dust with sugar, flavoured with a little ground cinnamon. Serve warm or cold.

Serves 8–10
Preparation time: about 1 hour, plus resting
Cooking time: 35–40 minutes

CRANBERRY POACHED PEARS

2 cups cranberry juice
¼ cup orange juice
½ cup sugar
I stick cinnamon
I star anise (optional)
4 firm, ripe pears
½ cup fresh cranberries

1 Put the cranberry juice, orange juice, and sugar in a saucepan large enough to hold the pears. Heat gently to dissolve the sugar. Add the cinnamon and star anise, if using, and boil for 5 minutes.

2 Peel the pears and immediately stand them in the pan with the cranberry syrup. Cover and simmer gently for 40 minutes, or until the pears are cooked and soft through to the center when pierced with a skewer.

3 Remove from the heat and leave to cool completely in the syrup. Chill for 2 hours or overnight, occasionally turning the pears in the syrup to achieve an even color.

4 Remove the pears from the pan and bring the cranberry syrup to the boil for 10 minutes, or until reduced to a thick syrup. Add the fresh cranberries and simmer for a further 5 minutes. Remove from the heat and set aside until completely cool.

5 Place the pears on a plate with the cranberries and pour the sauce over and around them.

Serves 4
Preparation time: 10 minutes, plus chilling
Cooking time: 1 hour

FRESH CRANBERRY CHEESECAKE

about 1¼ cups graham crackers, crushed
6 tablespoons superfine sugar
1 teaspoon ground allspice
6 tablespoons butter
1½ tablespoons apricot jam
2½ cups cranberries, defrosted, if frozen
3 large strips orange zest
¾ cup sugar

Filling:
1 tablespoon powdered gelatin
8 tablespoons orange juice
⅔ cup light brown sugar
2 tablespoons grated orange zest
1¾ cups cream cheese
1¾ cups ricotta cheese
½ cup heavy cream or whipped cream

1 Grease and line an 8-inch springform pan. Mix the crumb mixture with the superfine sugar and spice. Melt the butter and jam, and stir in to the crumb mixture. Press into the bottom and up the sides of the pan.

2 Place the cranberries in a saucepan and cover with water. Add the orange zest, bring to the boil, and simmer for 5 minutes. Stir in the sugar and leave to cool.

3 To make the filling, dissolve the gelatin in the orange juice in a bowl over a pan of simmering water, then stir in the brown sugar and orange zest. Add the cheeses and beat thoroughly. Reserve a little cream and fold the rest into the filling. Strain the cranberries through a strainer. Spread half the fruit over the base, cover with the filling, and finish with the remaining fruit and cream. Chill for 5–6 hours.

Serves 8
Preparation time: 45 minutes, plus chilling
Cooking time: 10 minutes

CRANBERRY-PORT SORBET

1½ cups cranberries, defrosted, if frozen
½ cup superfine sugar
1¼ cups orange juice
1 cup water
2 tablespoons port
2 egg whites

1 Put the cranberries, sugar, orange juice, and water into a saucepan, bring to the boil, cover, and simmer gently for about 20 minutes, or until the cranberries are tender.
2 Strain the mixture through a strainer, catching the juices in a bowl. Blend the cranberries in a liquidizer until smooth and add to the juices. Allow to cool, then add the port.
3 Pour the cranberry and orange mixture into a shallow container and freeze until 'slushy' around the edges. Whisk the egg whites until stiff but not dry.
4 Turn the semi-frozen sorbet into a bowl, break up the ice crystals, then fold in the whisked egg whites. Return to the container and freeze until firm. Scoop into glasses and serve.

Serves 4
Preparation time: 30 minutes, plus freezing
Cooking time: 30 minutes

FROZEN CRANBERRY MOUSSE

2 cups cranberries, defrosted, if frozen
2 tablespoons cranberry jelly or sauce
2 egg yolks
¼ cup superfine sugar
1 tablespoon orange liqueur
1½ teaspoons gelatin
2 tablespoons hot water
1 egg white
½ cup heavy or whipping cream

To decorate:
mint leaves
julienne strips of orange

1 Put the cranberries and cranberry jelly in a saucepan and heat gently for 5 minutes, stirring frequently, until the cranberries have softened. Purée in a blender or food processor until smooth. Cool.
2 Whisk the egg yolks and sugar together until pale and thick, then mix with the cranberry purée and orange liqueur.
3 Dissolve the gelatin in the water. Whisk the egg white until standing in dry peaks and the cream until softly peaking. Fold both the egg white, cream and dissolved gelatin into the cranberry mixture.
4 Divide the mixture between six ramekins and freeze for 2–3 hours, or until firm. Remove from the freezer 20 minutes before serving to soften. Decorate with mint leaves and strips of orange.

Serves 6
Preparation time: 25 minutes, plus freezing
Cooking time: 8 minutes

CRANBERRY ICE

1½ cups cranberry juice
½ cup superfine sugar
1 cup cranberries, defrosted, if frozen
3 tablespoons finely grated orange zest

To decorate:
sprigs of mint
sugar-frosted cranberries

1 Put the cranberry juice and sugar into a saucepan and heat gently to dissolve the sugar. Bring to the boil and simmer for 5 minutes. Remove from the heat, stir in the cranberries and orange zest and allow the mixture to cool completely.

2 Pour the mixture into a shallow container and place in the freezer until firm 1 inch around the edges. Turn the semi-frozen ice into a bowl, whisk well to break up the ice crystals, then return to the container and freeze until semi-frozen. Whisk once more, then freeze again until firm. Alternatively, pour the chilled mixture into an ice-cream machine and churn until thick and frozen. Transfer to a container and freeze until firm.

3 Remove from the freezer 15 minutes before serving and scoop into bowls. Decorate with mint and sugar-frosted cranberries.

Serves 4
Preparation time: 10 minutes, plus freezing
Cooking time: 10 minutes

APPLE & CRANBERRY CRUMB PIE

Pastry:
1½ cups all-purpose flour
pinch of salt
6 tablespoons butter, cut into small pieces
1½–2 tablespoons water

Filling:
9 ounces apples, peeled and thickly sliced
1½ cups cranberries, defrosted, if frozen
½ cup superfine sugar
1½ cups all-purpose flour
6 tablespoons butter
¾ teaspoon ground cinnamon
½ teaspoon grated lemon zest
½ cup light brown sugar

Liqueur cream:
1½ cups whipping cream
confectioner's sugar, sifted, to taste
orange liqueur, to taste

1 To make the pastry, sift the flour and salt into a bowl. Cut and rub in the butter until the mixture resembles fine bread crumbs. Add enough water to form a firm dough. Knead lightly until smooth and free from cracks.

2 Preheat the oven to 350°F. Grease an 8–9-inch springform tart pan. Roll out the pastry on a lightly floured surface then use to line the pan. Chill until required.

3 To make the filling, toss the apples and cranberries in the sugar and put them into the pastry shell.

4 Place the flour, butter, cinnamon, and lemon zest in a bowl, then rub together until crumbly. Stir in the brown sugar. Sprinkle evenly over the fruit and pat down lightly.

5 Bake for 45 minutes, or until the crumb topping and pastry are golden brown.

6 To make the liqueur cream, whip the cream until it begins to thicken. Sweeten to taste with confectioner's sugar and add a spoonful or two of the liqueur to taste, then continue whipping until the cream is thick and stands in soft peaks.

7 Serve the pie warm or cold, with the liqueur cream.

Serves 6–8
Preparation time: 20 minutes
Cooking time: 45 minutes

CRANBERRY-ORANGE GATEAU

2 eggs
½ cup superfine sugar
I cup all-purpose flour
1½ tablespoons grated orange zest

Filling:
1½ cups cranberries, defrosted, if frozen
⅔ cup orange juice
6 tablespoons superfine sugar
1½ cups heavy cream
2–3 tablespoons milk
3–4 tablespoons orange liqueur
½ cup slivered almonds, toasted
crystallized orange slices, to decorate

1 Preheat the oven to 350°F. Grease and line an 8-inch round cake pan with greased wax paper.

2 Whisk the eggs and sugar together in a large electric mixer or by hand, in a heatproof bowl over a pan of very gently simmering water, until very thick and pale in color, and the whisk leaves a heavy trail.

3 Sift the flour twice. Fold it lightly and evenly through the mixture with the orange zest. Turn into the prepared cake pan and level the top.

4 Bake for 25–30 minutes or until well-risen and just firm to the touch. Turn out on to a wire rack and leave until cold.

5 To make the filling, put the cranberries and orange juice into a saucepan, cover and simmer for 5–10 minutes, until the cranberry skins begin to pop. If necessary, boil uncovered for a few minutes, until thick and pulpy. Sweeten to taste with the sugar and set aside to cool.

6 To assemble the gâteau, whip the cream and milk together until stiff. Cut the cake in half horizontally and put the base on to a serving plate. Sprinkle with half the orange liqueur then spread with about three-quarters of the cranberry mixture and about a quarter of the cream. Top with the other cake layer and sprinkle with the remaining orange liqueur.

7 Put about a third of the remaining cream into a piping bag fitted with a star nozzle. Use the remainder to cover the gâteau completely. Swirl the cream on top with a round-bladed knife. Press the almonds all round the sides of the gâteau. Pipe cream around the top edge of the gâteau, then another circle a little in, leaving an empty space in the center. Carefully spoon the remaining cranberry filling into the center of the cream. Top with slices of crystallized orange. Chill the gâteau for 1 hour before serving.

Serves 6–8
Preparation time: about 1 hour, plus chilling
Cooking time: about 25–30 minutes

CRANBERRY MUFFINS

1 egg
6 tablespoons milk
6 tablespoons butter or margarine, softened
1¼ cups all-purpose flour, sifted
3 teaspoons baking powder
6 tablespoons superfine sugar
⅔ cup frozen cranberries, partially defrosted

Topping:
2 tablespoons superfine or confectioner's sugar
1 teaspoon cinnamon

1 Preheat the oven to 350°F. Grease and flour 2–3 muffin tins (15 cups).

2 Whisk together the egg and milk. Beat in the softened butter or margarine.

3 Sift together the flour and baking powder and stir into the mixture with the sugar. Mix thoroughly until smooth, then add the cranberries, folding them in gently.

4 Spoon the mixture into the muffin tins, filling them three-quarters full. Mix the topping ingredients together and sprinkle over the muffins. Bake for 20 minutes, or until firm to the touch. Let the muffins cool in the tins for 2–3 minutes, then turn them out and serve immediately.

Makes 15
Preparation time: 10 minutes
Cooking time: 20 minutes

CRANBERRY-ORANGE MUFFINS

½ cup finely chopped cranberries, defrosted, if frozen
5 tablespoons sugar
2 teaspoons grated orange zest
I cup all-purpose flour
I teaspoon baking powder
¼ teaspoon salt
I egg, beaten
¼ cup sour cream
¼ cup orange juice

1 Preheat the oven to 400°F. Grease 1–2 muffin tins (12 cups).
2 Mix the cranberries with 2 tablespoons of the sugar and the orange zest, then set aside.
3 Sift the flour, baking powder, and salt into a bowl and add the remaining sugar. In another bowl, beat the egg, sour cream, and orange juice together with a few swift strokes. Quickly fold in the cranberry mixture.
4 Spoon the batter into muffin tins, filling them two-thirds full and bake for 18–20 minutes, or until risen and golden brown. Let the muffins cool in the tins for 2–3 minutes, then turn them out and serve immediately.

Makes 12
Preparation time: 10 minutes
Cooking time: 18–20 minutes

CRANBERRY, CHOCOLATE CHIP, AND OATMEAL COOKIES

¼ cup butter
¼ cup sugar
¼ cup light brown sugar
I egg, beaten
¼ cup all-purpose flour
¼ cup oatmeal
¼ cup plain chocolate chips
2 tablespoons dried cranberries

1 Preheat the oven to 350°F. Grease two baking sheets.
2 Beat the butter and sugars together until soft and fluffy. Add the egg, flour, oatmeal, and chocolate chips and mix together until smooth.
3 Place about 16 large spoonfuls of the mixture, 2 inches apart, on the baking sheets. Scatter dried cranberries over each spoonful. Bake in the oven for 10 minutes, or until the cookies begin to brown around the edges but the centers remain soft. Do not overcook or the chocolate will burn.
4 Leave to cool on the baking sheets for 15 minutes before transferring to a wire rack to cool.

Makes 16
Preparation time: 15 minutes
Cooking time: 10 minutes

CRANBERRY BUNDT CAKE

6 ounces butter
1 cup brown sugar
2 eggs, beaten
1¼ cups cake flour
2 teaspoons baking powder
½ teaspoon ground allspice
¼ cup sour cream
grated zest of 1 lemon
¼ cup chopped mixed peel
1 cup roughly chopped cranberries, defrosted, if frozen
confectioner's sugar, for dusting

1 Preheat the oven to 350°F. Grease and line a 9-inch cake pan with wax paper.

2 Beat the butter and sugar together until soft and fluffy. Add the beaten eggs, little by little, beating well in between each addition. Sift the flour with the baking powder and allspice and stir into the cake mixture with the sour cream.

3 Add the lemon zest, mixed peel and cranberries and mix together. Spoon into the prepared pan and cook on the middle shelf of the oven for about 1 hour, or until a skewer inserted in the center of the cake comes out clean.

4 Leave the cake to cool in the pan, then turn out on to a wire rack and dust heavily with confectioner's sugar.

Serves 12
Preparation time: 20 minutes
Cooking time: 1 hour

CRANBERRY SMOOTHIE

½ cup cranberries, defrosted, if frozen
3 tablespoons sugar
½ cup water
2 cups plain yogurt
1 cup coconut milk

To serve:
cracked ice cubes
mint sprigs
cape gooseberries
fresh cranberries

1 Put the cranberries, sugar, and water into a saucepan and heat gently to dissolve the sugar. Bring to the boil and cook for 5 minutes. Remove the pan from the heat and allow to cool completely.

2 Put the cranberry syrup in a blender or food processor with the yogurt and coconut milk and blend until smooth.

3 Divide the smoothie between four tall glasses filled with cracked ice and serve decorated with a sprig of mint, and a cape gooseberry and a fresh cranberry threaded on to a cocktail stick.

Serves 4
Preparation time: 10 minutes, plus cooling
Cooking time: 5 minutes

CRANBERRY CRUSH

crushed ice
3 pints sweetened cranberry juice
1 pint fresh orange juice
1 pint ginger ale
orange and lemon slices, to decorate

1 Half fill a large punch bowl with crushed ice. Pour in the cranberry and orange juices and stir to mix.

2 Add the ginger ale, stir, then decorate with orange and lemon slices. Serve immediately.

Makes 5 pints
Preparation time: 5 minutes

CRANBERRY SANGRIA

1½ cups dry red Spanish wine
2 tablespoons brandy
¼ cup fresh cranberry juice
1½ cups lemonade or carbonated
mineral water

To decorate:
½ orange, thinly sliced
½ lemon, thinly sliced
1 apple, thinly sliced
¼ cucumber, thinly sliced
ice cubes

1 Mix the red wine and brandy together in a large jug. Add the cranberry juice and lemonade or mineral water and stir well to mix. Chill in the refrigerator for about 2 hours.
2 Before serving, float the fruit and cucumber slices on top of the sangria and add a few ice cubes.

Makes about 1¼ pints
Preparation time: 10 minutes, plus chilling

SPICED MULLED WINE

½ **pint water**
¼ **cup superfine sugar**
I bottle claret
½ **pint sweetened cranberry juice**
I cinnamon stick, broken in half
6 cloves
¼ **pint brandy**
cinnamon stick, to serve (optional)

I Place the water and sugar in a large saucepan and heat gently, stirring, until the sugar has dissolved. Pour in the claret and cranberry juice and add the cinnamon and cloves. Slowly bring the mixture just to the boil, then remove from the heat and add the brandy.

2 Strain through a strainer and discard the spices. Serve in warmed heatproof glasses with a cinnamon stick in each glass, if liked.

Makes 2½ pints
Preparation time: 5 minutes
Cooking time: 10 minutes

THANKSGIVING PUNCH

I pint cranberry juice
I pint orange juice
¼ pint water
½ teaspoon ground ginger
½ teaspoon mixed spice
sugar, to taste

To decorate:
kumquats, sliced
frosted cranberries
mint sprigs

1 Place the juices, water, and spices in a saucepan and bring gently to the boil, stirring in sugar to taste. Simmer for 5 minutes.
2 Pour into punch cups and float kumquat slices on top and decorate with frosted cranberries and mint on cocktail sticks. You can also serve this drink chilled for a summer party.

Makes 2½ pints
Preparation time: 10 minutes
Cooking time: 5 minutes

FRUIT PUNCH

I pint orange juice
I pint cranberry juice
½ pint pineapple juice
8 fluid ounces soda water
ice cubes

To decorate:
orange slices, quartered
I apple, thinly sliced
pineapple chunks

1 Place the juices and soda water in a large punch bowl or jug and mix well. Leave to chill in the refrigerator until required.
2 Add ice cubes and decorate with fruit. Serve immediately.

Makes about 3 pints
Preparation time: 10 minutes, plus chilling.

CRANBERRY CHAMPAGNE FIZZ

crushed ice
cranberry juice
Champagne

Fill a tall glass with crushed ice, quarter fill with cranberry juice, then fill to the top with champagne.

Serves 1

CRANBERRY TEQUILA SUNRISE

ice cubes
1½ fluid ounces tequila
cranberry juice
fresh orange juice
1 tablespoon grenadine

Fill a highball glass with ice cubes and add the tequila. Pour in the cranberry and orange juices to within ½ inch of the top of the glass. Add the grenadine which will sink to the bottom of the glass and partially permeate the juice.

Serves 1

COSMOPOLITAN

1½ fluid ounces vodka
1½ fluid ounces cointreau
cranberry juice
lime juice
crushed ice
lime twist, to serve

Pour all the ingredients into a cocktail shaker with some crushed ice, shake thoroughly, pour into a cocktail glass, and serve with a lime twist.

Serves 1

CAPE CODDER

1½ fluid ounces of vodka
cranberry juice
1 teaspoon lemon juice
crushed ice
lemon twist, to serve

Pour all the ingredients into a cocktail shaker with some crushed ice, shake thoroughly, pour into a cocktail glass and serve with a lemon twist.

Serves 1

SEA BREEZE

1½ fluid ounces vodka
cranberry juice
pink grapefruit juice
crushed ice

Pour all the ingredients into a cocktail shaker with some crushed ice, shake thoroughly, pour into a cocktail glass, and serve.

Serves 1

CRANBERRY SPRITZER

1½ fluid ounces white wine
cranberry juice
crushed ice
1½ fluid ounces soda water
slice of lime, to serve

Pour the wine and cranberry juice over crushed ice in a tall glass, fill to the top with the soda water, and serve with a slice of lime.

Serves 1

CRANBERRY RUM FIZZ

3 fluid ounces dark rum
2 tablespoons cranberry juice
1½ teaspoons superfine sugar
soda water
crushed ice

Pour all the ingredients into a cocktail shaker with some crushed ice, shake thoroughly, and serve.

Serves 1

TANGERINES WITH CRANBERRY SAUCE

¼ **cup sugar**
½ **cup water**
½ **cup cranberry juice**
8 **large tangerines**
¼ **cup fresh cranberries**
3 **tablespoons orange liqueur**
sprig of mint, to garnish

1 Put the sugar and water in a saucepan and heat gently until the sugar has dissolved. Bring to the boil and continue to boil for 5 minutes until the syrup becomes a golden caramel. Put the base of the pan into cold water to stop the caramel darkening further.

2 Add the cranberry juice to the pan and heat gently to dissolve the caramel into the cranberry juice.

3 Remove the skin and pith from the tangerines. Using a sharp knife, cut the pith from the zest of two of the tangerines then, using a very sharp knife, cut the zest into julienne strips. Add these to the caramel with the peeled tangerines and gently simmer in a covered pan for 10–15 minutes, turning frequently. Do not over cook.

4 Remove the tangerines from the syrup and bring the syrup to the boil for 10 minutes or until thickened. Add the fresh cranberries, remove from the heat, cool, and add the orange liqueur. Pour over the tangerines and chill until required. Garnish with a sprig of mint.

Serves 4
Preparation time: 25 minutes, plus chilling
Cooking time: 30 minutes

CRANBERRY SAUCE

3 **cups fresh cranberries**
1½ **cups sugar**
2 **teaspoons grated orange zest**
1 **cup water**

1 Place the cranberries, sugar, orange zest and water in a saucepan. Bring the mixture to a boil. Skim off the foam, lower the heat, and simmer for 5–10 minutes, or until the cranberry skins begin to pop. Remove from the heat and pour into a bowl. Let the mixture cool completely. Cover with clingfilm and refrigerate until ready to serve.

Serves 8–10
Preparation time: 5 minutes
Cooking time: 5–10 minutes

BRANDIED CRANBERRY SAUCE

1¼ cups cranberries, defrosted, if frozen
¼ pint water
2 tablespoons light brown sugar
a little grated orange zest
2 tablespoons brandy

1 Place all the ingredients in a saucepan. Cook, covered, over a low heat, stirring, for 5–10 minutes, until the cranberry skins pop.
2 Serve hot, in a sauceboat.

Serves 6
Preparation time: 5 minutes
Cooking time: 5–10 minutes

SPICED CRANBERRY JELLY

2 pounds cranberries, defrosted, if frozen
2 pounds cooking apples
4 oranges, sliced
3½ pints water
1 cinnamon stick
2 mace blades
½ teaspoon cloves
½ teaspoon allspice berries
about 4 cups sugar
fresh cranberries, to decorate

1 Place the cranberries in a large saucepan. Cut the apples into pieces and add to the pan. Add the oranges and pour over the water. Stir in the cinnamon, mace, cloves, and allspice and bring to the boil. Simmer gently for about 45 minutes, or until the fruit is very soft.
2 Strain through a jelly bag and leave to drip for at least 2 hours, or overnight. Measure the juice, pour into a large saucepan, and bring to the boil. Add 2 cups of sugar for every 1 pint of juice. Heat gently, stirring until the sugar is dissolved. Bring to the boil, then boil rapidly until setting point is reached (see page 62). Remove the scum immediately and pour into hot, sterilized jars. Add a fresh cranberry to each jar, seal and label.

Makes approx 5 lbs
Preparation time: 15 minutes, plus straining
Cooking time: 50–55 minutes

CRANBERRY RELISH

I large orange
I pound cranberries, defrosted, if frozen
I cup sugar
2 firm pears, peeled, cored, and diced
⅔ cup red wine vinegar
2 teaspoons salt

1 Pare the zest from the orange in long pieces, then cut into fine strips. Place in a saucepan with the cranberries, sugar, and pears.
2 Squeeze the juice from the orange and make up to ½-pint with the vinegar. Add to the pan with the salt. Heat gently, stirring until the sugar is dissolved, then simmer for 10–15 minutes until the fruit is just tender. Pour into hot sterilized jars, then seal and label.

Makes about 1½ pounds
Preparation time: 10 minutes
Cooking time: 15–20 minutes

SPICED CRANBERRY AND APPLE CHEESE

2 pounds cranberries, defrosted, if frozen
2 pounds cooking apples, chopped
¾ cup grated orange zest
⅓ cup orange juice
I teaspoon cloves
I cinnamon stick
2 mace blades
I pint water
about 4 cups sugar

1 Place the cranberries, apples, orange zest, orange juice, and the spices in a saucepan. Pour the water over and cover the pan. Bring to the boil, then simmer for about 30 minutes, or until the fruit is soft and pulpy. Rub through a strainer and weigh the purée.
2 Return it to the pan and add 1 cup of sugar for every 1 pound of purée. Stir over a low heat until the sugar has dissolved. Continue to cook, stirring, until the purée is very thick. To test if cooked, draw a spoon across the bottom of the pan – it should leave a clean firm line through the mixture. Pour immediately into hot, sterilized, oiled jars or moulds. Cover with plastic wrap, and seal as for jam. Keeps for 1 month, or 3 months in the refrigerator.

Makes about 4 pounds
Preparation time: 10 minutes
Cooking time: about 1½ hours

CRANBERRY JAM

2 pounds cranberries, defrosted, if frozen
½ pint water
1½ pounds sugar

1 Place cranberries and water in a saucepan, then bring to the boil. Reduce the heat and simmer until the fruit is soft and pulpy.
2 Add the sugar, bring to the boil again, stirring until the sugar has dissolved. Boil rapidly until setting point is reached. To test for setting point boil to 220°F and check the temperature with a sugar thermometer or cool one teaspoon of jam on a saucer. A skin should form which wrinkles when pushed with a finger. Skim.
3 Pour the jam into hot sterilized jars. Cover.

Makes about 3 pounds
Preparation time: 5 minutes
Cooking time: 1 hour

CRANBERRY SALSA

1 cup cranberries, defrosted, if frozen
1 red onion, chopped
½ cup canned pineapple, chopped
½ tablespoon sugar
1 tablespoon freshly chopped Italian flat-leaf parsley
2 tablespoons lime juice
1 firm avocado
salt and pepper

1 Put the cranberries, half the red onion, half the pineapple, and the sugar in a blender or food processor and blend to a rough purée.
2 Spoon into a bowl with the remaining red onion, pineapple, parsley, and lime juice. Season to taste. Mix together well and leave to stand at room temperature for 20 minutes before using.
3 Just before serving, peel and dice the avocado and add to the mixture. Check the seasoning.

Makes 2 cups
Preparation time: 15 minutes, plus standing

INDEX

64